The Next Great Awakening

How to Empower God's People with a Coach Approach to Ministry

Coach Training Leader's Guide

J. Val Hastings, MCC

Phone: 877.381.2672

Email: val@coaching4todaysleaders.com

Website: www.coaching4todaysleaders.com

ISBN # 978-0-9964837-0-4

Published in the USA

Table of Contents

Introduction

The vision of Coaching4Clergy is that every spiritual leader has coach training in their professional toolkit. Your participation in this Train-the-Trainer event is helping this vision become a reality.

Whatever (or whoever) motivated you to take this next step, I want to thank you. You are beginning a journey that will add tremendous value to pastors and churches everywhere.

Our coach training program is not primarily a lecture presentation. It is intentionally designed to be a combination of teaching, demonstrating and hands-on experiential learning.

The learning environment also includes large and small group learning experiences.

It is our belief that learning happens over the breaks, as well as in the actual sessions. That's why there are ample breaks and suggested topics for participants to consider over the break time.

A key understanding and assumption with this training is that each of your participants will have their own copy of the book. You are not teaching the workbook page by page, rather the training event is about bringing the book to life.

We want to be attentive to all types of participants, including extroverts, introverts and tactile learners. We provide ample opportunity for the extrovert to jump into the conversation and ask questions. We also consider the introverts, by providing them with information ahead of time, giving them questions and information over a break to prepare, as well as making space for them by sometimes prefacing questions with: "Before you answer this question, I want everyone to take about 30-60 seconds to think this through." Pipe cleaners, or something similar, are available at each table for those that learn best when their hands are moving.

30-day follow-up calls and a complimentary coaching call after the training help further cement the learning and new discoveries of the two days of coach training.

One last note: You'll want to select a coachee for each of the live coaching demonstrations ahead of time. Ask them to bring a real situation from their life.

SCHEDULE OVERVIEW

DAY ONE	
Topic	**Time**
Welcome and Introduction	10 min.
1. WHAT IS COACHING	50 min.
~ Break~	10 min.
2. DEEP LISTENING	1 hour 10 min.
~ Break~	10 min.
3. POWERFUL QUESTIONING	30 min.
~ Lunch ~	60 min.
4. COACHING PRACTICE	1 hour 5 min.
~ Break~	10 min.
5. ARTFUL LANGUAGE	35 min.
~ Break~	10 min.
6. ACTION AND ACCOUNTABILITY	45 min.
Wrap Up	15 min.
TOTAL TIME	**7 hours**

SCHEDULE OVERVIEW (con.)

DAY TWO	
Topic	**Time**
Welcome and Introduction	10 min.
1. LIVE Coaching Demonstration	45 min.
~ Break~	10 min.
2. THE COACHING RELATIONSHIP	1 hour 10 min.
~ Break~	10 min.
3. THE COACHING AGREEMENT	35 min.
~ Lunch ~	60 min.
4. COACHING LAB	1 hour 30 min.
~ Break~	10 min.
5. CREATING NEW AWARENESS	30 min.
~ Break~	10 min.
6. DIRECT COMMUNICATION	15 min.
Wrap Up	25 min.
TOTAL TIME	**7 hours**

TRAINING OUTLINE - DAY ONE

Time	Topic	Instructions/Content	Resources
5 min.	Welcome and Introduction	Brevity is the key. They will learn more about you throughout the day.	
5 min.	Overview of the day	Quick review of agenda (distribute copies of the agenda). Go over the schedule of breaks and lunch. Hospitality issues.	
	1. WHAT IS COACHING		
25 min.	Live coaching demonstration	Set the stage for the coaching demonstration by asking the group to go on mute. They will have an opportunity to ask questions. Make sure that all participants can hear and see you and the coachee. Treat this like a REAL coaching situation.	
15 min.	De-brief the live coaching demonstration	First, debrief the coachee. Ask them what it was like to be coached, as well as what might be different if they were regularly coached. Invite the observers to share observations and ask questions. Use the observers' comments and questions to transition into the topics: • What is coaching? • How is coaching different from therapy, consulting and mentoring? • Why does coaching work? • What would be different if you were regularly working with a coach? (Be sure all of these questions are covered during the discussion.)	
5 min.	Why does coaching work?	DKDK, KK, KDK, DKK learning model: • DKDK—Don't know that I don't know • KK—Know that I know • KDK—Know that I don't know (20-40% retention and application) • DKK—Don't know that I know (60-80% retention and application)	PowerPoint slides
5 min.	Questions and comments		
10 min.	Break	Ask them to think of any further questions or comments over the break. Introverts will appreciate that you have given them time to reflect on what they've heard.	
5 min.	Post-break	Discuss any questions or comments that came up over the break.	

Time	Topic	Instructions/Content	Resources
	2. DEEP LISTENING		
10 min.	Introduction to Listening	Read aloud from three different sources and ask the participants which piece was the easiest to listen to and which was the most challenging. Discuss their responses and transition the discussion to make the point that everyone will find it easier and more difficult to listen to certain people. Invite the participants to pair up or form triads, and discuss when it's easier or more challenging to listen. Also ask them to brainstorm about steps they can take to make it easier. Bring the groups back together and ask a few people to share their discoveries. Discuss the concept that "all coaching begins with listening" and why they might believe it to be true.	A children's story (I use *The Cat in the Hat*) A job description from the Help Wanted section A piece of poetry
5 min.	What is listening?	Have the group discuss their definition, and share these sample phrases: • Being curious • Quieting your mind • Creating a safe space for another person • Exploring possibilities • Giving another person your full attention • Reflecting back • Really "getting" (understanding) another person	
5 min.	Listening research	Senior managers saved 62% of their time when they were all given the opportunity to be listened to. Ask the participants to discuss how their own ministry settings would benefit from everyone listening and being listened to. Share this Native American proverb: If you want to know someone, walk a mile in their shoes—but first take off your own shoes. (Deep listening requires us to set aside our own agenda and ego.)	*Time to Think* by Nancy Kine
5 min.	How we communicate	90% of our communication happens non-verbally 7% happens verbally (3% is unknown)	
5 min.	What a coach is listening for	Listen to what the other person is saying, as well as what they are not saying. Listen from deep within (gut-level listening). Listen to "get" the other person.	

Time	Topic	Instructions/Content	Resources
		(Continued from previous page)	
	What a coach is listening for	Listen without judgment, criticism or agenda. You are creating a safe place for the person to share.	
		Listen without thinking about what you will be saying next.	
		Listen for values, frustrations, motivation and needs.	
		Listen for the greatness in the person you are coaching.	
		Listen for limiting beliefs and false assumptions. What does this person really believe the outcome or future will be?	
		Listen for shoulds, oughts and musts. They are frequent indicators of obligation and guilt versus what the person really wants.	
		Listen for the obvious. What is the other person not seeing or not aware of?	
		Listen for the tone, pace, volume, inflection and frequently used words. Also, notice when these change.	
		Listen for the larger context.	
		Listen attentively to the end of the statements. The best words often flow out last as well!	
		Listen to your reactions as you listen.	
30 min.	Listening exercise	Instruct the group to listen deeply as you speak, listening for some of the things we identified above.	Topics: What it was like growing up in my house.
		Suggest they practice "selective listening," honing in one or two specific things in the list.	Ways I have changed over the years.
		For 2-3 minutes, speak about one of the topics in the right-hand column. Be real, but brief.	My plans for the next few years.
		When you have finished, asked the participants to share what they heard.	The funniest thing that ever happened to me.
		Comment and coach them on what they are sharing.	
		Have the participants divide into pairs or triads and take turns discussing one of the topics in the list for 3 minutes.	
		Give the listeners 5-10 minutes to share what they heard, and what it was like to give another person their full attention.	
		Give the speakers 5-10 minutes to share what it was like to have another person's full attention.	
5 min.	Questions and comments	Before the break, let people know that the focus after the break will be on powerful questions, and ask them to think about what makes a question powerful.	
10 min.	Break		

Time	Topic	Instructions/Content	Resources
	3. POWERFUL QUESTIONING		
20 min.	Questioning exercise	Inform the participants that for this exercise you will be sharing a real situation from your life and that you want them to listen deeply and begin to think about questions to ask you. Instruct them to initially ask you questions that are <u>not</u> helpful at all. They are to ask you questions that would make you feel guilty or distract you. After the group has had the opportunity to ask many questions that are <u>not</u> helpful, make the following statement: *Congratulations! You have convinced me that you are all experts at asking questions that are not helpful. And, because you are experts at asking non-helpful questions, I know that you can also become experts at asking really great questions.* Now ask the participants to ask you questions that are helpful. As participants offer questions, talk about what made each question helpful and powerful. Begin to wrap up this exercise by asking the following question: Based on this exercise and our group discussion, WHAT MAKES A QUESTION POWERFUL? Develop and unpack their responses. Here are examples of what makes a question powerful: • Open-ended. • Present-focused versus past- or future-focused. • Free of judgment, shame and manipulation. • A direct result of deep listening. • Laser-focused and to the point. • Evocative of discovery or a new perspective. • Clarifying. • Action-oriented.	
3 min.	Powerful questions in the Bible	There are multiple examples of powerful questions in the Bible. Refer to the following: The Genesis story with Adam and Eve hiding in the garden after eating the apple. God asks them: Why are you hiding? Jesus and the healing of the man by the pool of Bethsaida. Jesus asks him: Do you want to be well? His response —No one puts me in the pool when the water is stirred. (He is blaming others.) Jesus tells the man to get up and carry his bed. He gets up and carries his bed.	Scripture: Genesis 3:9 and John 5:6

TRAINING OUTLINE - DAY ONE (con.)

Time	Topic	Instructions/Content	Resources
	Powerful questions in the Bible	*(Continued from previous page)* Discuss the following questions: • Why did God/Jesus, who is all knowing, ask this question? • What makes the question that God/Jesus asks powerful? • In your current role as a pastor, ministry staff or church leader when would a powerful question be most beneficial? • What impact would powerful questions have in your ministry setting?	
2 min.	Additional resources and materials	• Val's Favorite Questions • Top Ten Year-End Questions • Top Ten Questions for Leaders	Appendix A
5 min.	Questions and comments from the participnts		
60 min	Lunch	Inform the participants that after lunch we will be dividing into pairs to coach each other. Everyone will coach and everyone will be coached. Over lunch participants are to identify a topic they will be coached on. The topic must be a <u>real</u> and <u>current</u> situation for them. Invite participants to review the coaching model over lunch.	Coaching model from coach training manual.
50 min.	4. COACHING PRATICE	Quickly review the model: • Listen • Evoke • Clarify • Brainstorm • Support Give participants the following directions: Pair up. Everyone is coached and everyone coaches. Each person coaches for 15 minutes. Debrief for 5 minutes. Then switch roles.	Coaching model and graphic from coach training manual.
15 min.	Debrief the coaching practice	Use the following questions with the large group to debrief the practice coaching: • What was it like for you to coach? • What was it like for you to be coached? • What further questions do you have?	
10 min.	Break	Tell the participants that after the break we will be on focusing on artful language.	

TRAINING OUTLINE - DAY ONE (con.)

Time	Topic	Instructions/Content	Resources
5 min.	5. ARTFUL LANGUAGE	Make a few statements about language: *Sticks and stones may break my bones, but words will never harm me. NOTHING IS FURTHER FROM THE TRUTH!* Mark Twain said, *"The difference between the right word and the almost right word is the difference between lightening and a lightening bug."* He is so right! Language is like the brush in an artist's hand—an art form in its own right. Your choice of language is crucial in your ministry setting.	
20 min.	Language exercise	Language exercise: "Yes, but…" versus "Yes, and…" Two volunteers are needed for this fun exercise. Ask specifically for people who would be willing to "ham-it-up." Ask the two volunteers to select a topic from a list of topics that you have offered. Instruct the two participants to have a back-and-forth conversation about the topic they selected. Each person should purposefully respond with an opposing view and open their sentences with "Yes, but…" After a few minutes of this discussion, ask them to continue the conversation, but this time opening their contrary statements with "Yes, and…" After completing the exercise, ask the group what they noticed in this language exercise. Ask the volunteers what difference that one word made in their conversation.	Sample topics: Government Inflation Celebrities in the news
10 min.	Additional language exercises	Coaches use clean language. Language that is free of judgment, assumption, ego, and shame. Clean language exercise: Ask participants to respond to these statements in ways that are not clean. Then clean them up. • I'm ready to take my church to the next level. • I always feel like I'm the referee in my family. • It's been a long day. **Alignment:** Coaches also align, or purposefully misalign, their language when coaching. Discuss with participants various ways to align their language with someone they are coaching. Also discuss the benefits and dangers of aligning language, as well as when would you want to intentionally misalign your language with another person. **Distinctions:** Coaches also use distinctions, which are similar words or phrases that have subtle differences. These differences, when noted, can make a world of difference. Review the list of distinctions from the coach training book.	Artful language section of the coach training manual. *The Art of Possibility* by Ben Zander.

Time	Topic	Instructions/Content	Resources
	Additional language exercises	*(Continued from previous page)* **Acknowledgement** is another component of language that is central to the coaching process. Consider that: • Most people find it easier to list their weakness versus their strengths. • We need five acknowledgements to counter the effects of every one perceived criticism. **Acknowledgement exercise:** Ask participants to turn to someone near them and describe how someone has recently acknowledged them. Have them discuss what that was like; what lasting impact did it have? Bring the group back together and have a few people share their small group discussion. **Acknowledgment example:** Describe Ben Zander's strategy of every student getting an "A" at the beginning of the semester, and the amazing difference this approach makes. Ask the group: • What would it take for you to see others as an "A"? • How different would your ministry setting be if seeing others as an "A" was the norm?	
10 min.	Break		
5 min.	6. ACTION AND ACCOUNTA-BILITY	This session addresses the three components of this building block: • Brainstorming • Designing the action • Support and follow-through	
10 min.	Brainstorming exercises	Engage the large group in a brainstorming activity such as: • **9 dots:** Ask the participants to draw nine dots on a page, in the same shape as a Tic-Tic-Toe game. Now challenge them to connect the nine dots without lifting their pen from the page. • **Pipe cleaners:** Give your participants at each table 60 seconds to work as a group to create something out of the pipe cleaners (already placed at each table). Ask the group to discuss how, when problem-solving, we quickly develop patterns of thinking and behavior AND stop seeing other options. In coaching, this shows up in the temptation to jump right into designing the client's action plan. This limits us! When we intentionally brainstorm on our own or with coachees, we open ourselves up to different ways of being, thinking and behavior. Quote: "Nothing changes if nothing changes."	

TRAINING OUTLINE - DAY ONE (con.)

Time	Topic	Instructions/Content	Resources
15 min.	Designing the action	Introduce this next phase of the coaching model and reiterate that the brainstorming phase had to come first. Offer these helpful questions for designing the action plan: • Based on what we've talked about, what's your next step? • What's your vision? • What do you want to be able to say about this action 30 days from now? • What can you do today? Right now?	
15 min.	Support and follow-through	Many individuals and groups have a plan, but get side-tracked or derailed during the implementation phase. Action and accountability addresses implementation issues. Offer these helpful questions: • Where might you get derailed with this plan? • Based on previous experiences, what or who is likely to sabotage this plan? • Who can support you? • What kinds of support and accountability have been lpful in the past? • What will you report back to me the next time we talk?	
15 min.	Wrap up	Begin to wrap up Day One by addressing any questions or comments that students have. <u>If you are only doing a one-day event</u>, remind participants to complete their follow-up forms, sign up for a complimentary coaching call and attend the 30-day follow-up call. Also, review suggested next steps for their coach training. <u>If you are facilitating a two-day event,</u> give the participants a preview of the next day: a LIVE coaching demonstration, going over the remainder of the building blocks and giving everyone the chance to coach and be coached. Invite a couple of participants to briefly describe what they are taking away from this day. Close by thanking the participants and host.	

TRAINING OUTLINE - DAY TWO

Time	Topic	Instructions/Content	Resources
5 min.	Welcome and Introduction	Brevity is the key.	
5 min.	Overview of the day	Go over the schedule of breaks and lunch, as well as any hospitality issues. Offer a brief review of Day One and a preview of Day Two. In the review, mention the four building blocks from day one: • Deep listening • Powerful questions • Artful language • Action and accountability Convey to the participants that today's training will be similar in process, with the exception that they will have several opportunities to practice coaching (everyone will have the opportunity to coach and be coached today). Briefly introduce the building blocks that you will cover today: • The coaching relationship • Coaching presence • The coaching agreement • Creating new awareness • Direct communication	Distribute copies of the agenda
25 min.	1. LIVE COACHING DEMONSTRA-TION	Set the stage for a LIVE coaching demonstration by asking the group to go on mute while you coach someone. Remind them that just like on Day One, they will have an opportunity to ask questions. Make sure that all participants can hear and see you and the coachee. Invite the observers to notice the building blocks you discussed on Day One, plus pay particular attention to the building blocks you're discussing today. Treat this like a REAL coaching situation.	
20 min.	Debrief the live coaching demonstration	First, debrief the coachee. Ask them what it was like to be coached, as well as what might be different if they were regularly coached. Then, invite the observers to share observations and ask questions. Use the observers' comments and questions to cover yesterday's four building blocks, plus today's additional four building blocks. Be sure all of these questions are covered during the discussion: • What did you observe about the relationship between the coach and coachee? What were your observations of how the coach intentionally developed the relationship?	

Time	Topic	Instructions/Content	Resources
	Debrief the live coaching demonstration	*(Continued from previous page)* • What was the agreement? How did the coach set the agreement? • What, if any, new awareness occurred? What was the coach's contribution to new awareness? • What struck you about the communication between the coach and coachee?	
10 min.	Break	Before the break tell the participants that the next segment will be about the coaching relationship. Invite them to reflect about a time when they related well to someone else.	
30 min.	2. THE COACHING RELATIONSHIP	Ask if any additional questions or observations about the LIVE coaching demonstration came to mind over the break. Briefly address these and then move into the coaching relationship. Initiate a conversation with the large group about a time when they related well to someone else, using these questions as a framework for the discussion: *What was present when you related well?* *What are the benefits of relating well?* *What is unique about the way in which a coach relates to a coachee?* Introduce these unique features of the coaching relationship, if they don't come up during the group discussion: • The relationship is safe. • In-to-me-see (intimacy) occurs. • The coach is 100% present to the person being coached. • The coach is listening 80% of the time versus speaking 20% of the time. • The coach is listening at multiple levels. • The coach is listening for the essence of the person or group. • Curiosity and interest are present. • The coach is an outside observer and doesn't get hooked on the coachee's situation. • The coach doesn't treat the person as someone who needs to be fixed. • The coach taps into the strengths of the coachee.	Use the group's common experience of the LIVE coaching demonstration as a resource you can refer back to when unpacking each building block.
15 min.	Smaller group discussion	Have the participants divide into smaller groups (3-5 in a group). Ask them to discuss what steps they can each take to further develop the way that they relate to other people – in coaching relationships or relationships in general. After 10 minutes, ask a few people to give "laser-like" reports about their possible next steps.	

TRAINING OUTLINE - DAY TWO (con.)

Time	Topic	Instructions/Content	Resources
25 min.	Large group discussion– Coaching presence	There is another unique feature of the coaching relationship called coaching presence. Coaching presence is the ability to be totally spontaneous, while also being fully present and in the moment. This total spontaneity involves a knowing that is beyond what is typically, or rationally, known and observed. It's similar to the athlete who can anticipate where the ball will be thrown, before it's thrown. Begin by tapping into the group knowledge base on this topic. The following questions will help begin the discussion: How do you access this deeper knowing? How do you further develop your own deeper level of knowing? Explore these methods: • Journaling. The act of writing helps many go deeper. • Personal care. It's hard to go deeper when you're barely managing life on the surface. • Prayer and meditation. Intentionally quieting oneself and tapping into the divine. • Scripture reading and study. • Risk. Share your hunches or gut feelings. • Listen from the heart versus head. Be intentional in shifting from intellect to intuition. Now, shift the discussion to the uses of coaching presence when coaching. The following questions will help begin this discussion: • What are ways as a coach to use this deeper knowing? • What role did coaching presence play in the earlier LIVE coaching session? The following are examples of the use of coaching presence: **Ask** – What are you feeling in your body right now? What might your body be trying to tell you? **Request** – What does your heart tell you? What does your intuition tell you? **Share** – I'm noticing something here, how about you? **Risk** – This is what I'm seeing right now: _________	Coaching relationship section of the coach training manual (example of Ginger Rogers and Fred Astaire)
10 min.	Break	Inform the participants that after our break we will be talking about the coaching agreement. We will also spend time talking about next steps for you in your coaching development.	
15 min.	3. THE COACHING AGREEMENT	Review the three components of the coaching agreement: • The initial coaching agreement • The ongoing coaching agreement • The evaluation of the coaching process	Coaching agreement section of the coach training manual

Time	Topic	Instructions/Content	Resources
	3. THE COACHING AGREEMENT	*(Continued from previous page)* Then review the coaching scenario located in the coaching agreement section of the book and cover the accompanying questions listed along with the coaching scenario. Invite participants to ask questions about the coaching agreement. If time permits, invite participants to pair up and practice setting the coaching agreement (it is more important to have time for the next segment, so that participants can use the lunch break to complete follow-up forms and consider next steps without feeling rushed). This will feel awkward and staged—ask them to practice this anyway. If time is limited you can always refer to the LIVE coaching demonstration and ask participants to briefly talk about what struck them about the coaching agreement in the LIVE coaching.	
20 min.	Next steps	Review the follow-up forms that you have distributed earlier. Cover each section and provide opportunity for students to ask questions. Request that they complete the form over the lunch break and return it to you. Suggest that they also sign up for one of our coaching groups and/or a complimentary coaching session. (You will have a sign-up sheet with dates/times for them to register while at the training.)	Sample follow-up forms from the Trainer Only section (Coaching4Clergy website)
60 min.	Lunch	Be available to answer questions. Also, inform participants that after lunch they will have the opportunity to coach and be coached. Ask them to think of a topic that they can be coached on. Their coaching topic must be REAL for them and current.	
90 min.	4. COACHING LAB	Invite the large group to divide into groups of two or three and explain that each person will have the opportunity to coach and be coached. When there are two in a group, each person will have up to 30 minutes to coach. After that, the two are to debrief the coaching process for approximately 15 minutes. Then, the two are to switch and repeat the process. When there are three in the group, each person will have up to 20 minutes to coach, and then the three are to debrief the coaching. They are to repeat this process so that each has the opportunity to coach. The debrief process that participants are to use is the sandwich process, beginning with a positive comment (the first slice of bread), followed by constructive feedback or questions about the coaching (the "meat") and finishing with another positive comment (the other	

TRAINING OUTLINE - DAY TWO (con.)

Time	Topic	Instructions/Content	Resources
	4. COACHING LAB *(con.)*	*(Continued from previous page)* slice of bread). The person who was the coach is the first to debrief, then the coachee, followed by the observer (in groups of three). Inform the participants that you are available to answer questions or assist coaches during the next 90 minutes. Let the participants know that you will also be walking around the room observing the coaching and may step in at times.	
10 min.	Break	Explain to the group that after the break you will debrief their coaching labs as a large group, and also explore the coaching skill of creating new awareness.	
10 min.	Large group	Debrief the coaching lab	
20 min.	5. CREATING NEW AWARENESS	Ask the group to define—in their own words—creating new awareness. Then spend the bulk of your time discussing how the coach facilitates new awareness. Let participants offer ideas, and then cover any of the following items that weren't included in the discussion: • Staying detached from the coachee's story • Evoking greater clarity • Tapping into their greatness • Working on fact versus feeling, or on trivial versus significant • Offering other perspectives • Being curious • Listening on multiple levels • Drilling down past the solution and getting to the shift. • Unearthing limiting beliefs and false assumptions End this session by offering a formula for addressing limiting beliefs. • What do you really, really want? • What are your beliefs about what you really want? • What is the positive opposite of this limiting belief? • If you knew this (the positive opposite) was true, what action would you take?	
10 min.	Break	Over the break, request that the participants practice interrupting each other. Also, inform the group that after our break the topic will be direct communication.	
15 min.	6. DIRECT COMMUNICA-TION	As you heard in Day One, coaches use language in an artful way. One of the ways that a coach uses language is what we call direct communication. Direct communication is: clear and laser, judgment free, timely and includes silence. In this session we are looking at four specific forms of direct communication: interrupting, advising, directing and messaging.	

Time	Topic	Instructions/Content	Resources
	6. DIRECT COMMUNICA-TION	*(Continued from previous page)* **Interrupting:** Ask people about their experience over the break, or in general, with interruption. Transition to discuss when it would be beneficial to interrupt a coaching client, and the best ways to do it. **Advising:** Remind participants that in a Top 10 list of what people wanted in a coach, #7 was advice, when appropriate and asked for. Explain that new coaches must first unlearn how to give advice before they can offer appropriate advice. Ask for examples of when it's best to offer advice. **Directing:** Directing is intentionally re-focusing an individual or a group back toward their goals. Directing is useful with an individual or group that frequently goes off on tangents or loses sight of their BIG goal. Having a coaching agreement in place is essential for directing. Examples of directing include: • Hold that thought and let's go back to.... • For the past several weeks we've focused on A,B,C. Is it time to move on to X,Y, Z? • Congratulations. Let's move on. **Messaging:** Messaging is about conveying a "truth" that must be understood in order for the individual or group to move forward, such as: • You are someone who is... • What I want for you is... • It's time for you to move from...to...	
25 min.	Wrap up	Begin the wrap up by asking for additional questions or comments from the group about the training that they have just completed. Remind participants about follow-up forms, signing up for a complimentary coaching call, the 30-day follow up call and the next steps for their coach training. Ask for a couple of volunteers to briefly describe their take-away from the two days of coach training. Congratulate the participants and thank them for their participation in this training event. Also, thank your host.	

HOW TO SUCCESSFULLY PROMOTE
YOUR COACH TRAINING EVENT

The Upside-Down Funnel Approach

Most people, when launching a business or an event, adopt something called the "funnel" approach. This approach, like a funnel, is wide at the top and narrow at the bottom. Using this approach, an individual attempts to contact, connect, network and market to as many people and organizations as possible. This approach attempts to touch a large number of people (wide end of the funnel) and usually yields a few people (narrow end of the funnel).

The Upside-Down Funnel Approach literally inverts the funnel—the traditional approach. Instead of a mass approach, which is very impersonal, this approach advocates connecting with a much smaller number of individuals and investing heavily in those relationships.

I contend that all that is needed in this 4-step approach are 4-7 people—really high-level contacts who I call your "connectors."

Step 1: Identify your connectors

Who are connectors? Where do you find them? Connectors are the individuals in your industry or organization who really know how to make things happen. Every organization has them. In history, think Paul Revere versus William Dawes. Both of these individuals were asked to spread the word about impending danger, but people listened to Paul and paid little attention to William.

One of my original connectors brought me 34 coachees all at once. Another connector has made it possible for me to be in front of hundreds of individuals year after year, plus connected me with other connectors. While not all of my connectors deliver this high volume of results at once, over time they have steadily helped me secure contracts, fill training events and meet other connectors.

To identify your connectors, sit down and begin listing names. Comb through your address book and contact list— they are in there. Remember, connectors are people that get things done, typically because they know a lot of people.

Step 2: Invest in your connectors

Connect with your connectors to develop your relationship further. Add value to their world by offering resources, such as tools, information or people who can help them. I've gotten to know many connectors by coaching them, befriending them and doing favors for them, and I can tell you this absolutely works—value is their currency.

Step 3: Be on the look-out for new connectors

I am always looking for my next connector. Early on I thought that connectors had to be people that I knew well, but that is definitely a myth. Connectors, by their very nature, like to expand their connections. It's what makes them so effective. I have several connectors that I have never met in person. They don't really know me, but they know another connector who recommended me.

Step 4: Bridge the gap for your connectors

Demonstrate to your connectors how your coach training event will fill a need for people in their network.

PROMOTIONAL TIME LINE AND CHECKLIST

3 months before your event

- Contact the host(s) of your event (telephone is best for your first contact, but email is fine for following up).
- Confirm the dates, times, location, room configuration and equipment needed:
    - PPT projector, screen, microphone, newsprint, laptop (unless you can bring your own)
    - Hospitality items that the host will provide, e.g., coffee, tea, snacks.
- Arrange for hotel and transportation to and from the event (ask your host for suggestions if needed).
- Ask your host to promote the event to individuals and organizations they believe would benefit from the event. Ask if there is anyone they would suggest you call directly.
- Contact additional connectors who will be able to help you promote your event.
- List your event on the Coaching4Clergy website.

1 month before your event

- Confirm with your host the configuration, equipment and hospitality items that you need.
- Ask if there are additional ways that you can be of assistance.

10-15 days before your event

- Check in with your host (email is fine).
- Compile your handouts and resources, such as:
    - Agenda
    - Pipe cleaners
    - Follow-up forms
    - Sign-up sheet for complimentary coaching sessions, including dates/times that you are available
    - Sign-up sheet for participants to register for group coaching
    - Handout with a list of dates, times and bridge line numbers of 30-day follow-up calls (with three or more options to choose from).
- Review your PowerPoint presentation.

2-3 days before your event

- Check in with your host. Provide your mobile number in case they need to contact you prior to the event. Confirm the time that you will arrive at the location and begin setting up.
- Review your roster.
- Finalize all of your handouts, props and sign-up sheets.

The day of your event

- Arrive early to set up.
- Place handouts by each seat.
- Place pipe cleaners by each section/table.
- Set up a glass or pitcher of water for yourself.
- Greet the participants as they arrive.

At the end of the day of your event

- Thank the host immediately after the event.
- Collect the follow-up forms and sign-up sheets.

PROMOTIONAL TIME LINE AND CHECKLIST (con.)

1-3 days after your event

- Call the host a few days later and thank them again.
- Forward a completed attendance roster and a copy of the follow-up form to Coaching4clergy. Retain a copy for yourself for follow up.
- Follow up and confirm dates and times with those who have requested a complimentary coaching session.

Within one week of your event

- Follow up on any requests or questions that participants have made
- Begin setting up any group coaching opportunities

30 days after your event

- Check in with your host.
- Prepare for your 30-day group calls (see below).
- Email participants with a reminder about the 30-day group calls, including the call details for each of the three or four possible dates.

After you've completed your 30-day groups calls and complimentary coaching sessions

- Send Coaching4Clergy a list of everyone who participated in a complimentary coaching call and/or a 30-day follow-up call. IMPORTANT: Coaching4Clergy must receive this documentation in order to issue a certificate of completion to any participant.

HOW TO FACILITATE A 30-DAY FOLLOW-UP CALL

55 minutes maximum

Welcome and thank you

- Thank everyone for being on the call
- Take attendance quickly by calling out each name
- Ask, "Can everyone hear me okay?"
- Explain conference call etiquette: when you want to speak, say your name, wait to be acknowledged by me and then share.

Today's objectives

- Explain that you are here to check-in regarding the coach training they received 30 days ago and any coaching that they've been doing since then, as well to further cement their learning from the event.
- Explain that you'll also be discussing the next steps that will continue to support and develop them as coaches

Part One

Two questions guide this section. Ask the first question, listen and respond. Then, after several participants have responded, ask the second question, listen and respond:

- What's working well in your coaching?
- Where do you need additional help? What are your challenges?

Part Two

Shift the conversation to next steps and offer to answer any questions. Be sure to cover the following topics:

- How to receive a certificate of completion
- How to be listed on Coaching4Clergy's Find-A-Coach website
- Additional training offered by Coaching4Clergy
- Individual or group coaching options at Coaching4Clergy

Closing the call

- Thank the participants again for attending the coach training that you facilitated 30 days ago, as well as for their participation on today's call.
- Invite them to contact you with any additional questions.

Printed in the USA
CPSIA information can be obtained
at www.ICGtesting.com
CBHW082303141024
15876CB00032B/871